HILARIO

DAD JOKES

So Bad, They're Actually Hilarious

Q: What did the zero say to the eight?

A: That belt looks good on you.

Q: What has more letters than the alphabet?

A: The post office.

Q: Why couldn't the bicycle stand up by itself?

A: It was two tired.

Q: What did one hat say to the other?

A: Stay here!
I'm going on ahead.

This graveyard looks overcrowded

People must be dying to get in.

I have a joke about chemistry,

but I don't think it will get a reaction.

Q: What concert costs just 45 cents?

A: 50 Cent featuring Nickelback!

Q: What does a bee use to brush its hair?

A: A honeycomb!

Q: Why did the math book look so sad?

A: Because of all of its problems!

Q: What happens when a strawberry gets run over crossing the street?

A: Traffic jam.

Q: What do you call a pony with a sore throat?

A: A little hoarse.

Q: What do clouds wear?

A: Thunderwear.

Q: How do you get a good price on a sled?

A: You have toboggan.

Q: What do you call a hot dog on wheels?

A: Fast food!

Q: How do lawyers say goodbye?

A: We'll be suing ya!

Q: Can February March?

A: No, but April May!

Q: Wanna hear a joke about paper?

A: Never mind—it's tearable.

Q: When does a joke become a dad joke?

A: When it becomes apparent.

Q: Why are elevator jokes so classic and good?

A: They work on many levels.

Q: What is the scariest tree?

A: BamBOO!

Q: Why do standup comedians perform poorly in Hawaii?

A: Because the audience only responds in a low ha.

Q: Why can't you send a duck to space?

A: Because the bill would be astronomical.

Q: I once got fired from a canned juice factory

A: Apparently I couldn't concentrate.

Q: Where do you find a cow with no legs?

A: Wherever you left it.

Q: Why did Karen press Ctrl+Shift+Delete?

A: Because she wanted to see the task manager.

Q: What language do people speak in the middle of the earth?

A: Core-ean

Q: Why are bakers so rich?

A: They make so much dough.

I'm really excited for the amateur autopsy club I just joined.

Tuesday is open Mike night!

Q: Why didn't the melons get married?

A: Because they cantaloupe.

Q: How did the pirate get his ship so cheap?

A: It was on sail.

Q: Did you hear about the cheese that's been working out?

A: Dude's shredded.

Q: What did the big flower say to the tiny flower?

A: Hey there bud!

My boss asked me why I only get sick on work days.

I said it must be my weekend immune system.

Whoever stole my depression medication:

I hope you're happy.

I've been thinking about taking up meditation.

I figure it's better than sitting around doing nothing.

I finally got around to watching that documentary on clocks.

It was about time.

Q: Why can't a leopard hide?

A: Because he's always spotted.

The world tongue-twister champion just got arrested.

I hear they're gonna give him a really tough sentence.

Q: What do you call a beehive without an exit?

A: UnBeeLeaveable!

So what if I don't know what apocalypse means?

It's not the end of the world.

Q: Why haven't aliens visited our Solar System yet?

A: They looked at the reviews... only 1 star!

Lost my job at the bank on my first day.

A woman asked me to check her balance, so I pushed her over.

Q: What do you call a typo on a headstone?

A: A grave mistake.

Q: hat do you call two octopuses that look the same?

A: Itenticle.

My wife told me to pick up 8 cans of soda on my way home from work...

She was pretty mad when I only picked seven up

Q: How do you tell the difference between an alligator and a crocodile?

A: You will see one later and one in a while.

I'll never tell my accountant a joke again.

He just depreciates them.

Q: Why do vampires have no friends?

A: They suck.

It hurts me to say this,

but ... I have a sore throat.

My psychiatrist says I have an unhealthy obsession with revenge.

We'll see about that...

I don’t trust those trees.

They seem kind of shady.

My wife said if I bought her one more stupid gift, she would burn it.

So i bought her a candle.

There was once a king who was only 12 inches tall!

Terrible king, but made a great ruler.

Q: Why did the spoon come to the party dressed as a knife?

A: The invitation said to look sharp.

The best gift I ever received was a broken drum.

You can't beat that.

Q: How did the barber win the race?

A: He knew a shortcut.

Q: What is the fastest growing city in the world?

A: Capital of Ireland. It's Dublin everyday.

Lost my job at the bank on my first day.

A woman asked me to check her balance, so I pushed her over.

Q: Did you hear about the kidnapping at school?

A: It's okay, he woke up.

I ordered a chicken and an egg online.

I’ll let you know.

I was going to tell a time-traveling joke,

but you guys didn't like it.

My wife is really mad that I have no sense of direction.

I packed up my stuff and right.

My boss told me to have a good day,

so I went home!

Q: Did you hear about the square that got into a car accident?

A: Yeah, now he's a rect-angle!

I have a joke about butter,

but I'm not going to spread it.

I have a joke about procrastination,

but I'll tell it to you later.

6:30 is my favorite time of day,

hands down.

Q: What do you call an illegally parked frog?

A: Toad.

Q: Do you know the story about the chicken that crossed the road?

A: Me neither, I couldn't follow it.

Q: What did the duck say when it bought chapstick?

A: Put it on my bill!

Q: What does a cow use to do math?

A: A cow-culator.

Q: Why do seagulls fly over the sea?

A: If they flew over the bay, they'd be called bagels.

Q: What did the big flower say to the tiny flower?

A: Hey there bud!

Q: What do frogs order at restaurants?

A: French flies.

Q: Where do cows go for entertainment?

A: To the moovies.

Q: Why was the calendar afraid?

A: Its days were numbered.

Q: What time did the man go to the dentist?

A: Tooth hurt-y.

Q: How do celebrities stay cool?

A: They have many fans.

Q: Why do you never see elephants hiding in trees?

A: Because they're so good at it.

Q: What do you call 50 pigs and 50 deer?

A: 100 sows and bucks.

Q: What do you call a donkey with only three legs?

A: A wonkey.

Q: What's blue and not very heavy?

A: Light blue

Q: What did the plumber say to the singer?

A: Nice pipes.

Q: Where do pirates get their hooks?

A: Second-hand stores.

Q: What do you call a line of men waiting to get haircuts?

A: A barberqueue.

Q: What do you call a can opener that doesn't work?

A: A can't opener!

Q: Which days are the strongest?

A: Saturday and Sunday. The rest are weekdays.

A buddy asked how many fish I caught.

I told him it's not polite to fish and tell.

A turtle is crossing the road when he's mugged by two snails.

When the police ask him what happened, the shaken turtle replies, "I don't know. It all happened so fast."

My IQ test results came back.

They were negative.

Stop looking for the perfect match.

Use a lighter.

My landlord told me we need to talk about the heating bill.

"Sure," I said. "My door is always open."

I love my furniture.

My recliner and I go way back.

Are you feeling cold?

Sit in the corner, it is 90 degrees.

Q: Wanna hear a joke about construction?

A: I'm still working on it.

Q: If a snake married a mortician, what would their bath towels say?

A: Hiss and Hearse.

Q: What's worse than biting into an apple and finding a worm?

A: Biting into an apple and finding half a worm.

As I get older, I remember all the people I lost along the way.

Maybe a career as a tour guide was not the right choice.

Q: What sort of room has no windows or doors?

A: A mushroom!

Q: What did the triangle say to the circle?

A: Your life has no point!

Printed in Great Britain
by Amazon

12835377R10031